Impressionists

Georges Seurat
1859–1891

Les impressionnistes, ces jeunes gens «en colère», ces «fous de lumière», ont remis en question les règles les mieux établies de l'art occidental, privilégiant la couleur, annonçant l'art moderne. En choisissant des sujets inusités, en inventant une technique nouvelle, ils ont provoqué la stupeur et le scandale. Il n'est pas d'usage, en effet, sous Napoléon III, d'atomiser les formes, de pulvériser les masses, de préférer la fragmentation de la touche et le contraste des couleurs au lisse, au fini, au léché des «Pompiers».

On peut se demander où commence et où finit cette révolte impressionniste dont on trouve les prémices chez Eugène Delacroix et J. M. W. Turner et dont les traces subsistent jusqu'à Henri Matisse et Pablo Picasso, Vassili Kandinsky et Jackson Pollock.

L'impressionnisme menait-il donc à tout, à condition d'en sortir? Peut-on parler de l'abstraction de Claude Monet, du cubisme de Paul Cézanne ou de l'expressionnisme de Vincent van Gogh? Lorsqu'ils reçoivent enfin la consécration du public, des critiques, des musées, les héros de cette aventure ont abandonné depuis longtemps toute référence à ce que l'on a appelé l'impressionnisme.

Henri de Toulouse-Lautrec
1861–1901

Il n'en reste pas moins que, par la magie de leur pinceau, des artistes, rassemblés peu de temps par une même passion (de 1860 à 1880 environ), mais chacun avec son génie propre, ont transformé notre vision du monde.

Désormais, la nature, les jeunes filles, un étang, une simple pomme ne seront plus tout à fait les mêmes.

Paul Gauguin
1848–1903

The Impressionists, those young »savages« preoccupied with light, challenged the firmly established rules of western art by elevating colour to a principle, thus setting the stage for the emergence of modern art. Their choice of subjects, misunderstood at the time, and the introduction of a new painting technique provoked outrage and scandal: it was not common in the days of Napoleon III to atomize forms and pulverize surfaces, emphasizing the vitality of the brushstroke and the evocative power of colour as opposed to the smooth, perfected, polished technique of the »conventionalists«.

It is difficult to define the scope of this Impressionist revolution, the origins of which go back to Delacroix and Turner and traces of which can be found in the work of Matisse and Picasso, Kandinsky and Pollock. Did Impressionism ultimately have an effect which was the opposite of what it set out to achieve? Can one speak in terms of abstraction in the works of Monet, of Cubism in those of Cézanne, or Expressionism in the case of van Gogh? The heroes of this adventure ultimately gained recognition among the public, the critics and the museums, and there is no longer any association with what Impressionism once was.

Be that as it may, each of these artists, driven for a short period of time (from 1860 to around 1880) by a common passion but marked by their individual genius, changed our way of looking at things with the magic of their brush strokes. Nature, young girls, a pond, a simple apple will never be the same again.

Edouard Manet
1832–1883

Claude Monet
1840-1926

Die Impressionisten, diese jungen »Wilden« – »versessen auf Licht«– stellten die fest etablierten Regeln der abendländischen Kunst in Frage, indem sie die Farbe zum Prinzip erhoben und so Wegbereiter der modernen Kunst wurden. Mit der Wahl damals noch unverstandener Themen und der Einführung einer neuen Maltechnik beschworen sie Empörung und Skandal herauf, denn zur Zeit Napoleons III war es nicht üblich, Formen zu atomisieren, Flächen zu pulverisieren, das Eigenleben des Pinselstrichs und die Ausdruckskraft der Farben dem Glatten, Vollendeten, Ausgefeilten der »manierierten Akademiker« vorzuziehen. Anfang und Ende dieser impressionistischen Revolution, deren Ursprung bei Delacroix und Turner liegt und deren Spuren bis hin zu Matisse und Picasso, Kandinsky und Pollock führen, sind schwierig abzustecken. Bewirkte der Impressionismus das Gegenteil von dem, was er ursprünglich wollte? Kann man von Abstraktion bei Monet, Kubismus bei Cézanne oder Expressionismus bei van Gogh sprechen? Finden die Helden dieses Abenteuers schließlich Anerkennung in der Öffentlichkeit, bei den Kritikern, den Museen, haben sie längst jeden Bezug zu dem, was einmal der Impressionismus war, verloren. Nichtsdestoweniger haben diese Künstler, die für kurze Zeit (von 1860 bis 1880 etwa) von derselben Leidenschaft besessen waren, jeder von ihnen jedoch mit seinem eigenen Genie, unsere Sicht der Dinge durch den Zauber ihrer Pinselführung verändert. Fortan sind die Natur, junge Mädchen, ein Teich oder ein einfacher Apfel nicht länger dasselbe.

Pierre-Auguste Renoir
1841–1919

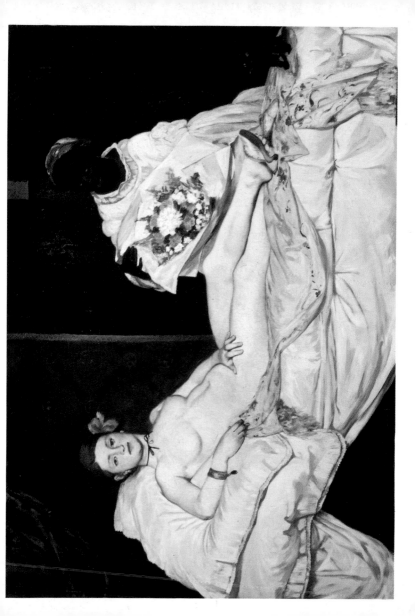

Edouard Manet: Une Botte d'asperges, 1880
Bundle of Asparagus / Ein Bündel Spargel
Cologne, Wallraf-Richartz-Museum

Claude Monet: Impression, soleil levant, 1872
Impression, Sunrise / Impression, Sonnenaufgang
Paris, Musée Marmottan

Claude Monet: La Japonaise (Camille Monet),
1875
Madame Monet in Japanese Costume / Camille
Monet im japanischen Kostüm
Boston, Museum of Fine Arts, Purchase Fund
1951, Courtesy Museum of Fine Arts

Claude Monet: La Promenade. La femme à l'ombrelle, 1875
Woman with a Parasol. The Walk / Der Spaziergang. Frau
mit Sonnenschirm
Washington (D.C.), National Gallery of Art.
Mr. and Mrs. Paul Mellon Collection

Claude Monet: La Cathédrale de Rouen, le portail et la tour
d'Albane à l'aube, 1894
Rouen Cathedral, Portal and Tour d'Albane in the Morning /
Die Kathedrale von Rouen am Morgen
Boston, Museum of Fine Arts, Tompkins Collection

© Benedikt Taschen Cologne PostcardBook

Claude Monet: Nymphéas, jadis Agapanthus, 1916-26
Water Lilies, formerly Agapanthus / Seerosen, früher
Schmucklilien
St. Louis, The Saint Louis Art Museum

© Benedikt Taschen Cologne PostcardBook

Edgar Degas: L'Etoile ou Danseuse sur la scène, 1876/77
The Star or Dancer on the Stage / Der Stern
Paris, Musée d'Orsay

© Benedikt Taschen Cologne PostcardBook

Paul Cézanne: Nature morte: Pommes et biscuits, 1879–82
Apples and Plate of Biscuits / Stilleben mit Äpfeln und Biscuits
Paris, Musée de l'Orangerie

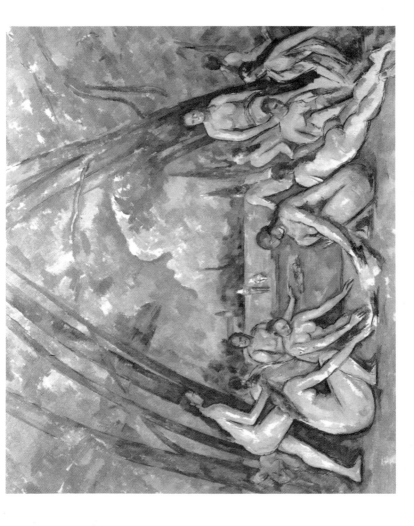

Paul Cézanne: Les Grandes Baigneuses, c. 1906
The Great Bathers / Die großen Badenden
Philadelphia, Philadelphia Museum of Art

Vincent van Gogh: Terrasse de café le soir, 1888
Café Terrace at Night / Terrasse des Cafés an der Place du
Forum in Arles am Abend
Otterlo, Rijksmuseum Kröller-Müller

Henri de Toulouse-Lautrec: La Goulue entrant au Moulin Rouge, 1892
La Goulue Entering the Moulin Rouge Accompanied by Two Women /
La Goulue betritt mit zwei Frauen das Moulin Rouge
New York, The Museum of Modern Art, Gift of Mrs. David
M. Levy

© Benedikt Taschen Cologne PostcardBook

Mary Cassatt: Petite Fille au fauteuil bleu, 1878
Little Girl in a Blue Armchair / Kleines Mädchen in blauem
Sessel
Washington (D.C.), National Gallery of Art,
Mr. and Mrs. Paul Mellon Collection

© Benedikt Taschen Cologne PostcardBook